NoLex 12/12

LAURA
WELCH
BUSH

LAURA
WELCH
BUSH

FIRST
LADY

TANYA LEE STONE

A Gateway Biography
The Millbrook Press
Brookfield, Connecticut

For Sarah, the First Little Lady of my life

Published by The Millbrook Press, Inc.
2 Old New Milford Road
Brookfield, CT   06804
www.millbrookpress.com

Library of Congress Cataloging-in-Publication Data
Stone, Tanya Lee.
Laura Welch Bush, First Lady / Tanya Lee Stone.
     p. cm. — (A Gateway biography)
Includes index.
ISBN 0-7613-2304-X (lib. bdg.) ISBN 0-7613-1539-X (pbk.)
 1. Bush, Laura Welch, 1946—Juvenile literature. 2. Presidents' spouses—United States—
Biography—Juvenile literature. [1. Bush, Laura Welch, 1946- 2. First ladies.] I. Title. II. Series.
E904.B87 S76 2001
973.931'092—dc21 [B] 2001018707

Cover photograph courtesy of Liaison Agency (© Rick Wilking)

Photographs courtesy of the Office of First Lady Laura Bush: pp. 10, 13, 15, 19, 26; AP/Wide
World Photos: pp. 14, 17, 38, 41; George Bush Presidential Library: p. 23, 25;
Liaison Agency: p. 27 (© Neil Schneider); Texas Rangers Baseball Club: p. 28; *Austin
American-Statesman*: p. 30; © AFP/Corbis: p. 32; Texas Library Association: p. 35; ©
SMU/Scott Langley: p. 37

LAURA

WELCH

BUSH

ON NOVEMBER 7, 2000, much of the United States population sat glued to their television sets. People were watching the results of the presidential election unfold. They expected to learn who the next president would be. But the process of counting all the votes was not finished by the time people went to sleep.

There was still no president-elect the next morning. Republican candidate George W. Bush was declared the winner in the early hours of the morning. Democratic candidate Vice President Al Gore had lost. But two hours later it was decided that the vote was still too close to call. How could this happen?

Some television stations had guessed what the final results would be. They made predictions before all the votes had been counted.

The race for the presidency was so close that everything depended on who had gotten the most votes in the state of Florida. And the number of votes for each candidate in Florida was so close that state officials had to recount the votes.

As the votes were recounted, people started taking a look at how the vote was held in Florida. Some people said they had trouble voting. Some said the places where they went to vote had closed too early. Others said the ballot was confusing. Those people thought they might have voted for the wrong candidate by accident.

Republicans and Democrats argued for several weeks. They were all trying to figure out how to choose the winner fairly. Both sides went to court over the issue. The presidential election was even brought to the highest court in America—the United States Supreme Court. This was the first time that had ever happened.

The election results were finally official on December 12, 2000. Out of the millions of votes that were cast for president, George W. Bush beat Al Gore by 537 votes. He is America's forty-third president. And his wife, Laura Welch Bush, is the nation's new First Lady.

Fifty-four years before the election that made his daughter America's First Lady, Harold Bruce Welch walked back and forth between his office and a nearby hospital. All day he waited for the important news. His wife, Jenna, was about to have a baby. He got the news he was waiting for at six o'clock in the evening. Their healthy baby girl was born on November 4, 1946. They named her Laura Lane Welch.

Laura grew up in the small town of Midland, Texas. Midland is in the western part of the state. Laura's father built houses. Her mother helped her father with the business. Laura learned the importance of helping others and caring for people from growing up in this small and friendly town. She loved

Christmas in Midland, Texas, brings a delighted four-year-old Laura a new doll and other presents.

to do the things that most kids love—play with her friends, ride her bike, and stare up at the big, blue Texas sky, daydreaming.

Laura always had a lot of friends. She was easygoing and kind. Everybody liked to go to Laura's house to play after school. Georgia Temple is one of her closest girlfriends from childhood. She describes Laura as "a good listener, quiet, but not shy, . . . a great sense of humor . . . and fun to be with." Life was full of simple pleasures for Laura. She enjoyed things like sleepover parties, sharing a soda with her friends, or taking a walk into town.

Laura knew she wanted to become a teacher when she was in second grade at James Bowie Elementary School. She used to play with her dolls and pretend she was their teacher. "Growing up, I practiced teaching on my dolls. I would line them up in rows for the day's lessons," Laura remembers.

She started as a Brownie Scout that same year. She was a Brownie from second grade to fifth grade. Then she became a Girl Scout. Laura's mother, Jenna, became a Scout Mother for the troop that same year. Laura continued as a Girl Scout until junior high. She went to Girl Scout Camp at Mitre Peak in Alpine, Texas. When Laura Bush became the First Lady in 2001, the Girl Scouts of the U.S.A. invited her to be their Honorary President.

Laura also sang when she was in grade school. She began at her family's church, First United Methodist, by singing in the Cherub Choir. She later moved into the older choir and sang until the end of junior high school. Laura also took piano lessons for about four years. And she had a lead part in the school play, "Caddie and the Indians," in fifth grade.

But Laura's favorite thing to do has always been reading. She remembers her mother having a lot to do with her earliest interest in reading. "My mother gave me a most precious gift—a lifelong passion for reading. When I was a child, she often took me to our local library in the basement of the Midland County Courthouse. . . ." And Laura's mother remembers the same. "I read to her from the time she was a baby. . . . As she got older, we read regular novels. . . ."

Laura and her mom, Jenna, in 1953

Laura read all the time, even when she was with friends. Gwyne Smith Bohren was a childhood friend of hers. She says, "I just remember we always did silly stuff on Friday nights when we spent the night together. And she [Laura] was always reading books." Laura Welch's favorites were the Little House on the Prairie books written by Laura Ingalls Wilder. One of

On the campaign trail one of the things Laura enjoys most is reading to kids.

her teachers first showed her the series. She fell in love with them. These books meant so much to her that she kept her whole collection and gave them to her daughters many years later.

Laura also had a passion for pets. A friend named Judy Jones Ryan gave Laura her first kitten when they were little girls. Ryan says, "I remember it had a real pug nose, kind of flat, and she would always push on its nose. It was a tabby. And she loved it and always loved cats from then on. . . " There were several other cats that came to live at the Welch's house. There was also a terrier dog named Bully.

After grade school Laura went to San Jacinto Junior High School. She didn't know that the man she

Here's a picture of Bully, the Welch family dog, with Laura at age two.

First Pets

A PRESIDENT's pets are often called the First Pets. George W. and Laura Bush's dog Spot has been training for this title since the day he was born. In fact, he was born in the White House. Spot's mother is a springer spaniel named Millie. She is the dog of former President George Bush and First Lady Barbara Bush. Millie gave birth to a litter of puppies in the beauty parlor of the White House on March 17, 1989. For the first few weeks of his life, Spot enjoyed running and jumping on the South Lawn of the most famous house in America.

Then Spot was given to George W. and Laura Bush. He moved to Texas to live with his new family. Spot lived in another famous house when George W. became the governor of Texas. He felt right at home in the governor's mansion. Spot reported to duty every morning at the Department of Public Safety at the mansion. These are the people who protect the governor's family. Spot patrolled the grounds with the guards and did his duty watching over his family. When his dad became president, Spot went back to the White House!

The First Family also has two cats. One of the cats is black. His real name is India, but the family calls him

Spot is catching a breeze in the backseat
as George and Laura drive around their ranch in
Crawford, Texas.

Willie. Their other cat, Ernie, was a stray cat that ended up on the lawn of the governor's mansion. Ernie is named after the author Ernest Hemingway. Hemingway had a six-toed cat, and Ernie has six toes. The First Family's newest pet is a Scottish terrier puppy. It was given to them a month before George W. was sworn in as president.

would marry was one of the boys in her class. Laura had other things on her mind. Laura decided where she wanted to go to college when she was in seventh grade. She read a book that told the life story of a football player named Doak Walker. Walker had gone to Southern Methodist University. Laura was sure SMU was the right college for her after reading that book.

But she still had her high school years ahead of her. Laura went to Lee High School. She was a quiet girl, but very popular. A friend named Regan Gammon recalls their high school days, "We just kind of hung out with our friends, listened to records, and drove around in cars drinking Cokes."

Laura traveled to Monterrey, Mexico, the summer after her sophomore year in high school. She went with some of her classmates to study Spanish. They had a wonderful time learning about the Mexican culture. One of Laura's friends who went along that summer was Jan Donnelly O'Neill. She remembers one thing they liked to do after class: "We'd come

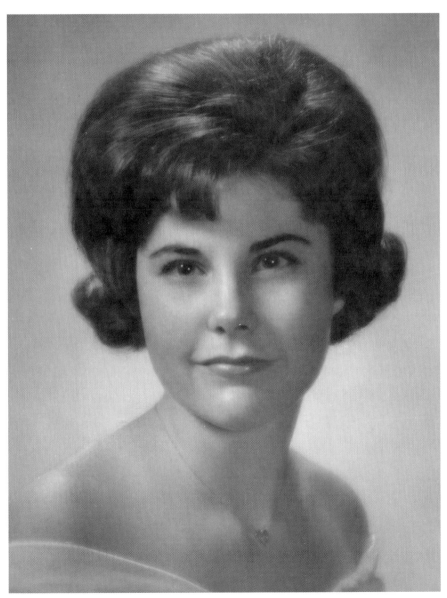

A portrait of Laura taken during her senior year of high school

back to the dorm and listen to the popular songs [on the radio] and try to figure out the lyrics."

Laura had a very peaceful and happy childhood growing up in a small Texas town. But there was one day that changed her life forever. A terrible accident took the life of one of her high school friends. Laura was seventeen. She was driving her car on November 6, 1963. She went through a stop sign and hit another car. The driver, a young man named Michael Douglas, was killed. No charges were filed against Laura.

The following year Laura Welch left her hometown to move to Dallas, Texas, for college. She was accepted to Southern Methodist University (SMU) just as she had hoped back in the seventh grade. Laura always wanted to be a teacher, so she took courses in education. She graduated with a bachelor's degree in education in 1968 and was ready to begin teaching.

THE SUMMER AFTER GRADUATION she got her first job as an elementary school teacher in Dallas. She taught there for one year. Then in 1969 she took a job as a second-grade teacher in Houston, Texas. Laura moved to a new city with three of her friends. She lived in a large apartment complex called the Chateau Dijon.

Once again, the man she would marry was right underneath her nose and she didn't know it. George W. Bush lived on the other side of the complex. They knew some of the same people but they never met. In George W. Bush's autobiography, *A Charge to Keep*, he remembers, "She lived on the quiet side of the Chateau Dijon; I lived on the loud side, where we played volleyball in the pool until late at night."

Laura taught for a few years. Then she decided to go back to school to become a librarian. She went to the University of Texas at Austin. There she studied for a graduate degree in library science.

She finished at the University of Texas in 1973 and moved back to Houston. Laura liked the city and wanted to be close to her friends. She got a job as a librarian at the Houston Public Library. But after about a year, she realized that she missed being around young children. She gave up her job at the public library. Laura moved back to Austin and took a job as the librarian at Dawson Elementary School.

Laura went home to Midland for a visit in the summer of 1977. Her friends, Joey and Jan O'Neill, invited her over for dinner. They wanted to introduce her to their friend George W. Bush. He had moved back home to Midland in 1975. The O'Neills had tried to have the two meet each other before. But Laura had always said no. She didn't think she would have much in common with a man who was interested in politics.

That all changed the minute they met. As now-President George W. Bush says, "We both love to read, we both love spending time with our friends, and we both, very quickly, fell in love with each other." The couple dated for three months. They married on November 5, 1977. It was a quiet wedding for family and close friends. Both Laura and George were thirty-one years old.

Laura Welch Bush left her job in Austin. She moved back to Midland to make a home with her new husband. Laura and George are very different from

A Bush family gathering for the wedding of George and Laura:
From left to right, Marvin, Dorothy, Neil, Columba, wife of Jeb,
who is to her left, Laura and George W., Barbara and George,
and Dorothy Walker Bush

each other. She is quiet and he can be loud. She is reserved and he is outgoing. Laura's mother-in-law, Barbara Bush, says, "Laura is the calm in George W.'s storm."

LAURA MARRIED INTO A WEALTHY and famous family. Her father-in-law was George H.W. Bush. He had been a congressman, a U.S. ambassador to the United Nations, and head of the Central Intelligence Agency (CIA). He later became the vice president and then the president of the United States. The man Laura had married, George W., had big dreams as well. He began campaigning to be a congressman right after the couple got back from their honeymoon. For a year they traveled all over Texas to meet voters. But George W. lost that election. Life went back to normal for a while.

Laura and George really wanted to have children. But for several years they were unable to. They decided to adopt a baby. A happy surprise came soon after that decision. Laura was pregnant with twins!

George's first run for public office began soon after he and Laura were married. Here they are meeting the voters Texas style in the back of a pickup truck.

She was sick during the last part of her pregnancy. Laura had to spend two weeks in the hospital. The doctors waited as long as they could so the babies could keep growing inside their mother.

One baby can seem overwhelming to a new mother, and Laura had two to take care of.

But the twins needed to be delivered five weeks before they were due. The baby girls were born on November 25, 1981. They were both perfectly healthy. They were named Barbara and Jenna, after each of their grandmothers. Their birth was big news in America because at that time their grandfather was the vice president of the United States.

George and Laura spent the next several years enjoying life with their daughters. George ran his own oil company. But something happened in 1986 that got George W. fired up about politics again. His father called the family together at Camp David. Camp David is a presidential retreat in Maryland.

Vice President Bush was planning to run for president. George W. was asked to help with the campaign.

George W. and Laura attend the Inaugural Ball for his father on the evening of January 20, 1989.

Laura and George moved their family from Midland to Washington, D.C., to be part of the team. George W.'s father won that election. He became the nation's forty-first president on January 20, 1989. The new president's son learned a lot about politics as he worked alongside people who had been in politics all their lives.

Not only did the girls get to go to the Rangers games, but they also got to sit in the dugout.

Laura and George did not want to stay in Washington, D.C. They wanted to get back home to Texas. The family moved to Dallas. In the spring of 1989, George W. Bush became one of the owners and managing partners of a major-league base-

ball team, the Texas Rangers. "George had always dreamed about owning a baseball team," Laura said. George and Laura took the girls to baseball games all the time. George loved managing the team. But after a few years he wanted to run for political office again.

His father's term in the White House had ended in 1993. George then felt free to run his own campaign. He started to talk about running for governor of the state of Texas. Laura was a little surprised that her husband wanted to give up the job he loved so much. But the more he talked about his ideas on how to make Texas a better place, the more she understood. The couple decided it was the right thing for their family.

On November 8, 1994, Laura's husband won the election. He became the forty-sixth governor of Texas.

George Herbert Walker Bush, Jenna, Barbara, Laura, and George W. during a moment of prayer at the 1994 inauguration.

The Bush family moved into the governor's mansion in Austin. Laura didn't enjoy speaking in public or being in the spotlight. But as First Lady of Texas her life was about to change a lot. She did a good job of keeping her daughters' lives private. And she became more comfortable talking to both crowds and reporters. She also found ways to get involved in things she cared about. Laura Bush quietly made a big difference in Texas.

Her mother-in-law, Barbara Bush, had been the First Lady of the United States. Laura had seen first-hand how Barbara had tackled literacy—the ability to read—as a main cause. Laura knew this was her chance to work at something she felt strongly about. During the six years she lived in the governor's mansion, Laura Bush put her heart into literacy and education projects. Her Early Childhood Development Initiative supported four main programs: the Family Literacy Initiative, Reach Out and Read, Texas Ready to Read, and *Take Time for Kids* parenting magazine.

Laura Bush created the First Lady's Family Literacy Initiative for Texas in 1996. She had some help from the Barbara Bush Foundation for Literacy. The goal of Laura's project is to support programs to help families learn to read. The Family Literacy Initiative has given fifty programs throughout Texas almost $1 million. Laura Bush is very happy about the results. "Parents tell us they've learned creative new ways to help their children develop language and reading skills, such as writing out shopping lists together, reading road signs when driving in a car, or

A Second First Lady

LAURA BUSH is not the first woman in her family to become the First Lady. Her mother-in-law, Barbara Bush, was the nation's First Lady from 1989 to 1993. Barbara Bush is married to George Herbert Walker Bush, who was the forty-first president of the United States. Now their son, George W. Bush, is the forty-third president.

This is the second time in American history that a father and son have both become president. In 1796, John Adams became the second president of the United States. Twenty-nine years later, his son, John Quincy Adams, was elected the sixth president.

Having two First Ladies in one family is remarkable enough. But Laura and Barbara Bush have even more in common. Both women have a love of books and often send each other books to read. And helping people learn to read is a big part of their lives.

Laura worked hard for this cause as the First Lady of Texas. And she has made it clear that, as First Lady of the United States, she plans to keep working. She wants more and more people to know the joy of reading.

Barbara Bush at a ceremony honoring her daughter-in-law in August 2000

playing 'teacher,'" she reported on her website when she was the First Lady of Texas.

Reach Out and Read is a national program for infants and toddlers. Doctors and nurses at Boston City Hospital started it. The purpose of the program is to give all children the chance to love books and learn to read. Under Reach Out and Read, part of a child's visit to the doctor includes being read to and being given books to take home. Any parents who cannot read are encouraged to sign up for a literacy course. They are also given tips on how to get their kids interested in reading. Through Laura Bush's efforts, there are now more than forty sites in Texas that offer Reach Out and Read to families with children.

Governor Bush signed a bill that gave $2 million to support the Texas Ready to Read program on June 17, 1999. Ready to Read helps thousands of low-income children in preschool with beginning reading skills such as learning letters and letter sounds. "This . . .

FUN FACT
The First Lady's favorite hobbies are reading and gardening.

give[s] Texas children the best possible start for a life-time of learning," Laura Bush said about the program.

Take Time for Kids is a parenting magazine that Laura Bush worked on with childhood-development experts and the Texas Department of Health. *Take Time for Kids* is put out in both English and Spanish because there are a lot of Spanish-speaking families who live in Texas. The magazine gives parents information they need about children's health and early-childhood learning.

Laura has encouraged reading in other ways as well. She joined Texas celebrities such as Chuck Norris and children's book author Pat Mora to help the Texas Library Association in 1998. The First Lady of Texas appeared on a poster entitled "Read For Your Life" that invited people to visit libraries and read.

Laura Bush also created the Texas Book Festival. This major event is held every year. Laura started it in 1996 with the help of the Texas Library Association, the Austin Writers League, and the Texas State Library. From 1996 to 2000, she served as the honorary chairwoman. Authors gather in Austin each year for the festival. They hold book signings and read from their books. Kids are a big part of the festival,

READ

for your life.

The library
wins big with
Laura Bush.

First Lady of Texas, Laura Bush

Texas Library Association

The Texas Library Association used celebrities from Texas to promote reading. Laura Bush was a natural choice for them.

too. They can hear stories told by their favorite authors, have their books autographed, watch jugglers, and make bookmarks. The festival raises money for Texas public libraries to buy more books.

In April 1999, Laura's husband gave her a wonderful present in honor of all the work she has done for literacy. George W. Bush had a beautiful walkway built at Southern Methodist University, just outside of the library. The path is lined with trees and is called the Laura Bush Promenade.

As the First Lady of Texas, Laura Bush also supported the arts. She served on the Texas Board for the National Museum of Women in the Arts. She worked with the Texas Capitol Historical Art Committee to collect art showing Texas heroes. The works are displayed in the Capitol building for visitors to see.

On June 7, 2000, Laura and George W. Bush welcomed twelve young artists to Austin. They were selected to have their artwork hung in the Capitol building. Laura Bush chose the twelve pieces from a hundred student works of art shown in the Youth Art Capitol Exhibition. "Millions of people visit the Texas Capitol every year, and I'm glad they have a chance to

The dedication ceremony for the walkway at Southern Methodist University that George had built. It's called the Laura Bush Promenade.

see the student art that is on display in the governor's business office," said Laura Bush when the children were honored.

Laura Bush also has worked to help organizations in the fight against breast cancer. She has helped the Susan G. Komen Breast Cancer Foundation, the

George W. Bush being sworn into office for his second term as governor of Texas with Laura, Jenna, and Barbara looking on.

American Cancer Society, and the Texas Health Department. October is Breast Cancer Awareness Month. In October 1998, Laura helped spread the message that finding breast cancer early is the best way to fight the disease. At an event called Tell-a-

Friend Friday she said, "Take a moment every Friday this month to encourage five of your friends to get a breast exam or mammogram."

Life was good for the Bush family in Texas. George W. was a very popular governor. Laura was well loved as the First Lady of Texas. And their daughters were enjoying a normal teenage life. They went to high school in Austin and often had friends over to the mansion. But there were even bigger things ahead for the family. In 1998 people started talking about George W. as a candidate for United States president.

Being the governor's wife was one thing. But this quiet girl from a small town had never dreamed of being the president's wife.

Laura was a little worried about how much their lives would change if George W. became president. She and George had always protected their kids from reporters. They wondered if they could continue to do that in the White House.

But the couple already knew a little about presidential life from former president George Bush. "We knew that [they] were still able to be wonderful parents to their children, and to have some private life, even in the White House," Laura says. George W. and Laura Bush decided to go for it.

The presidential campaign was in full swing in 1999. George W. was becoming well known all over the country. Laura went with him many times on the campaign trail. Public speaking didn't seem to bother her anymore.

The couple was busy with both the campaign for president and taking care of state business in Texas. Laura also needed to make time for her family. She needed to spend time helping her daughters get ready for college. They both headed off for their first year of college during the campaign. Jenna started at the University of Texas. Barbara went to Yale, just as her father and grandfather had done.

Laura joked about juggling both things and getting used to her daughters leaving home. She said in her

Laura and her girls, all dressed up for the inaugural ball on January 20, 2001.

speech at the Republican National Convention on July 31, 2000, "They say parents often have to get out of the house when their kids go off to college because it seems so lonely. . . . But I told George I thought running for president was a little extreme."

The race for the presidency was hard. George W.'s main rival was Vice President Al Gore. The nation was divided in their choice. The election was very close. About half of the country voted for George W. The other half voted for Al Gore. In the end, George W. won by 537 votes.

On December 12, 2000, the world learned that George W. Bush was America's next president. George W. was inaugurated—sworn into office—on January 20, 2001. And Laura Welch Bush became the First Lady of the United States. She has set some goals for herself as First Lady. "I have a lifelong passion for introducing children to the magic of words," she said. "I am proud of my efforts on behalf of the children of Texas, and I look forward to building those efforts on behalf of all American schoolchildren."

Important Dates

November 4, 1946	Laura Lane Welch is born
May 26, 1968	Laura Welch receives her bachelor's degree from Southern Methodist University
August 25, 1973	Laura Welch receives her master's degree in Library Science from the University of Texas at Austin
November 5, 1977	Laura Welch marries George W. Bush
November 25, 1981	Jenna and Barbara Bush are born
January 20, 1989	George Herbert Walker Bush becomes America's forty-first president
November 8, 1994	Laura Welsh Bush becomes First Lady of Texas
December 12, 2000	George W. Bush wins presidential race
January 20, 2001	Laura Welch Bush becomes First Lady

Sources

Allen, Jodie T. "In Philadelphia, the Spouse that Scored." *U.S. News & World Report*. August 14, 2000.

Anderson, Lisa. "Laura Bush: Stepping into the Spotlight." Chicago *Tribune*. August 1, 2000.

Arnold, Laurence. "Whitman Gives Bushes a Puppy, Terrier Will Pick Up Where Buddy Left Off." Associated Press, December 20, 2000.

Author interview with Mrs. Jenna Welch. December 14, 2000.

Barta, Carolyn. "Laura Bush Accepts SMU Award." Dallas *Morning News*, October 29, 1999.

Bilyeau, Nancy. "Meet the Next First Lady: Laura Bush." *Good Housekeeping*. October 2000.

Blyth, Myrna. "Fighting for the Family." *Ladies Home Journal* Online, November 2000.

Bonnin, Julie. "What Laura Wants." Austin *American-Statesman*. April 18, 1999.

Bush, Barbara. *Millie's Book: As Dictated to Barbara Bush*. New York: William Morrow, 1990.

Bush, George W. *A Charge to Keep*. New York: William Morrow, 1999.

Bush, Laura. Speech at The Republican National Convention on Monday, July 31, 2000.

Casey, Kathryn. "The OTHER Mrs. Bush." *Ladies Home Journal*. September 1999.

Cohen, Daniel. *George W. Bush: The Family Business*. Brookfield, CT: Millbrook Press, 2000.

Connelly, Joel. "Laura Bush Speaks Out From the 'Fishbowl.'" Seattle *Post-Intelligencer*. February 25, 2000.

Eagen, Margery. "Campaign 2000: This Year, May the Best Ladies' Man Win." Boston *Herald*. October 3, 2000.

Fikac, Peggy. "Laura Bush, Cancer Survivors Kick Off Campaign." Associated Press, October 3, 1998.

Hanchette, John. "Laura Bush: Shy No More." *USA Today*. June 23, 2000.

Hollandsworth, Skip. "Reading Laura Bush." *Texas Monthly*.

Koslow, Sally. "The First Wives Club." *McCall's*. October 2000.

"Laura Bush: 'The Calm in George W.'s Storm.'" Associated Press. March 3, 2000.

Mitchell, Alison. "A Political Wallflower Has a Full Dance Card." *The New York Times*. September 21, 2000.

Official website of the Office of the Governor of Texas.

Peppard, Alan. "Mrs. Bush Lets Down Her Guard." Dallas *Morning News*. March 24, 2000.

Pooley, Eric. "How George Got His Groove." *Time*. June 21, 1999.

Reaves, Jessica. "Now Making Her Bow: The Un-Hillary." Time.com. December 21, 2000.

Roiphe, Katie. "Married to the Job." *The Guardian*. September 20, 2000.

Schindehette, Susan, and Jerome, Richard. "Laura Bush: A Quiet Source of Strength." *People*. October 9, 2000.

Sciolino, Elaine. "Laura Bush Sees Everything in its Place, Including Herself." *The New York Times*. January 15, 2001.

"Talking with Laura and Barbara Bush." Cokie Roberts interview that aired on *This Week with Sam Donaldson and Cokie Roberts* on ABC, December 19, 1999.

Temple, Georgia. "Childhood Friends Say Laura Bush Loved Books, Scouting." Midland *Reporter-Telegram*. July 2000.

———. "Jenna Welch 'Extremely Proud' of Potential First Lady." Midland *Reporter-Telegram*. July 2000.

———. "Journalist Recalls Childhood Memories of Laura Bush." Midland *Reporter-Telegram*. July 2000.

———. "Laura Bush Reflects on Years in Midland." Midland *Reporter-Telegram*. July 30, 2000.

Thorpe, Helen. "George W.'s Gender Gap." *Harper's Bazaar*, January 2000.

Wehrman, Jessica. "Laura Bush: The Candidate's Steadying Influence." Scripps Howard News Service. November 23, 1999.

"Zone of Privacy: Some Issues are Not Relevant to Elections." Dallas *Morning News*. May 5, 2000.

INDEX